**W9-AOL-792**

 WITHDRAWN

J
0
P

Kid Pick!

Title: _____

Author: _____

Picked by: _____

_____

Why I love this book:

_____

_____

_____

POISON DART FROG

TAMRA B. ORR

Published in the United States of America by Cherry Lake Publishing
Ann Arbor, Michigan
www.cherrylakepublishing.com

Content Adviser: Dr. Stephen S. Ditchkoff, Professor of Wildlife Ecology, Auburn University, Alabama
Reading Adviser: Marla Conn, ReadAbility, Inc.

Photo Credits: ©reptiles4all/Shutterstock Images, cover, 1, 14, 21; ©Lennard Janson/Shutterstock Images, 5; ©IUCN (International Union for Conservation of Nature), Conservation International & NatureServe. 2010, 6; ©nikitsin.smugmug.com/Shutterstock Images, 7; ©Dirk Ercken/Dreamstime.com, 9; ©Dirk Ercken/Shutterstock Images, 11, 13, 17, 25; ©Dorling Kindersley/Thinkstock, 12; ©Alfredo Maiquez/Shutterstock Images, 15; ©Jdsf2/Dreamstime.com, 18; ©Erik Mattheis/http://www.flickr.com/CC-BY-SA 2.0, 22, 23; ©Vilainecrevette/Shutterstock Images, 27; ©ElenaMirage/Thinkstock, 28

Library of Congress Cataloging-in-Publication Data

Orr, Tamra, author.
    Poison dart frog / Tamra B. Orr.
    pages cm. — (Exploring our rainforests)
    Summary: "Introduces facts about poison dart frogs, including physical features, habitat, life cycle, food, and threats to these rainforest creatures. Photos, captions, and keywords supplement the narrative of this informational text."— Provided by publisher.
    Audience: Ages 8-12.
    Audience: Grades 4 to 6.
    Includes bibliographical references and index.
    ISBN 978-1-63188-977-6 (hardcover) — ISBN 978-1-63362-016-2 (pbk.) — ISBN 978-1-63362-055-1 (pdf) — ISBN 978-1-63362-094-0 (ebook) 1. Dendrobatidae—Juvenile literature. 2. Frogs—Juvenile literature. [1. Poison frogs.] I. Title.

    QL668.E233O77 2014
    597.87'7—dc23   2014021000

Cherry Lake Publishing would like to acknowledge the work of
The Partnership for 21st Century Skills. Please visit www.p21.org
for more information.

Printed in the United States of America
Corporate Graphics

ABOUT THE AUTHOR

Tamra Orr is a full-time writer and author living in the gorgeous Pacific Northwest. She loves her job because she learns more about the world every single day and then turns that information into pop quizzes for her patient and tolerant children (ages 23, 21, and 18). She has written more than 350 nonfiction books for people of all ages, so she never runs out of material and is sure she'd be a champion on Jeopardy!

TABLE OF CONTENTS

CHAPTER 1

Jewels of the Rainforest

Deep in the rainforest, scattered among the brown and green leaf litter on the floor, are bright drops of color. These colors stand out sharply against the plants and trees all around them. Look, there's orange and red! Over there, a glimpse of yellow. Under the tree is a sudden flash of green and blue. Tiny spots and stripes flicker between tree branches and the canopy of leaves. They hop, jump, and crawl. What are they?

Meet the "jewels of the rainforest"—poison dart frogs. They are tiny creatures, often no bigger than a

Poison dart frogs all have bright colors.

RANGE MAP

RANGE OF STRAWBERRY POISON FROG

Strawberry poison frogs live mainly in Costa Rica.

These frogs' toes help them climb on plants.

fingernail. More than 100 **species** make their homes
in the jungles of South and Central America and on a
few islands of Hawaii. Thanks to very sticky toes, they
are able to crawl across the forest floor. They also can
climb up tall trees to reach the safety of the overhead
leaves.

These frogs come in an incredible rainbow of
colors, including bright shades of orange, red, blue,
green, purple, and yellow. Some have striped patterns.
Others have spots.

In the wild, bright colors mean "Danger! Be careful! There's trouble ahead." For you, the clue is in these animals' name: *poison* dart frogs. They cannot bite or sting, so what is their hidden weapon?

On the brightly colored skin of these little **amphibians** is a type of slippery slime. It may look shiny and pretty, but don't be fooled. That shine is really a kind of venom, or poison. Any animal foolish enough to try to take a bite of these frogs is in for a big surprise! Not only will the poison make the frogs taste terrible, but even a single bite can be fatal!

Many species have such powerful poison that **predators** may die if they try to munch on the frogs. These jewels of the rainforest may be dangerous to touch, but they are fascinating to watch. ➤

Poison dart frogs have four toes on each of their front feet.

LOOK AGAIN

THE POISON DART FROG'S FEET AND TOES ARE DESIGNED TO KEEP THEM FROM SLIPPING WHENEVER IT CLIMBS TREES. CAN YOU THINK OF OTHER ANIMALS THAT HAVE FEET LIKE THIS?

CHAPTER 2

A Colorful Family

Have you seen frogs swimming at local ponds or in home aquariums? The 100 species of poison dart frogs have a lot in common with them. For one thing, poison dart frogs are shaped like most other frogs.

Frogs have very long back legs that fold up when they are sitting. These legs are strong. They straighten out when the frogs jump or hop. A frog's front feet have four toes. Its back feet have five. On the bottom of each toe are pads like suction cups that help the frogs grip the surface when crawling on the ground or climbing trees.

Poison dart frogs have very long back legs.

BODY DIAGRAM

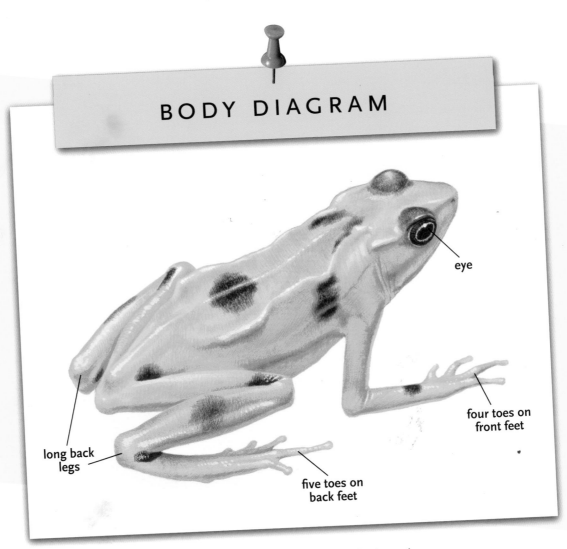

eye

four toes on
front feet

long back
legs

five toes on
back feet

Poison dart frogs have perfect bodies for jumping.

[21ST CENTURY SKILLS LIBRARY]

While all poison dart frogs are tiny, they still come in different sizes. They can be as small as 0.75 inches (2 centimeters) to as large as 3 inches (7.6 cm) long. The tiniest poison dart frog of all is called the Buzzer. It looks like a bumpy strawberry and is bright red. It makes a sound like a cricket. Another red frog is known as a strawberry poison dart frog. It has earned the nickname of "blue jeans" because of the dark-blue coloring on its back legs.

This is a strawberry poison frog.

The golden dart frog is the most dangerous frog in the world.

Golden poison dart frogs measure 1 inch (2.54 cm) long and weigh less than 1 ounce (28 grams). These bright-yellow frogs have black eyes and black-tipped toes. They are the most dangerous dart frogs in the world. They are only found in a small area of the rainforest on the Pacific coast of Colombia. One touch of its skin is enough to **paralyze** and kill tens of thousands of mice or a dozen human beings.

The blue poison dart frog is bright blue, with black spots and patches on its head and back. Amazingly, it was not discovered until 1968 in a tiny part of the rainforests in the Central American country called Suriname. Like a number of its cousins, the blue poison dart frog is on the edge of becoming **endangered**. Humans are often a threat to the habitats of these frogs as are natural dangers like forest fires.

Even though it's tiny, this poison dart frog is extremely dangerous.

LOOK AGAIN

How can you tell this frog is not able to swim? Hint: Look between its toes.

CHAPTER 3

PASSING ALONG THE POISON

The poison dart frog is hungry. It has spent the last hour hopping around the rainforest floor in search of a tasty snack. What looks good to these frogs? Insects! The frogs are able to notice the slightest movements in the grasses, leaves, and branches of the forest. They look closely, watching for signs of an ant, termite, beetle, fruit fly, spider, or other small insect to nibble.

Wait! There is a delicious-looking cricket. The frog takes aim. Zap! Out comes its long, sticky tongue. It wraps around the insect and pulls it back to its mouth

The shiny substance on this frog is poison.

to gobble it up. Yum! The **prey** is just what the frog had hoped to find for its afternoon meal.

Do any creatures hunt these colorful frogs? Thanks to the venom on the frogs' skin, they have very few predators. Any animal foolish enough to try to snap up a poison dart frog for dinner will regret it. Its muscles will stop working. Its stomach will hurt. If it manages to survive at all, the animal will have learned its lesson. Leave those nasty-tasting frogs alone!

The only animal able to include these frogs in its diet is a snake known as the fire-bellied snake. This fiery black, orange, and red snake is **immune** to the frog's poison! How does it do it? Experts are not quite sure. They think something in the snake's **saliva** stops the poison from working.

Different-colored frogs often live in the same areas of the rainforest.

The food the poison dart frogs eat does more than fill up their hungry stomachs. Their food is actually what lets them produce the toxic slime on their skin! Scientists have not yet figured out which insects are responsible for the poison. But they think it is a combination of the toxins found in various ants and beetles living in the rainforest. Poison dart frogs born and raised in zoos or kept in aquariums never become poisonous. Perhaps the saying "You are what you eat" is especially true for these frogs.

GO DEEPER

HOW DOES THE FOOD CHAIN IN THE RAINFOREST SHOW HOW ONE SPECIES DEPENDS ON ANOTHER TO SURVIVE?

CHAPTER 4

GOING FOR A PIGGYBACK RIDE

Listen! There is a buzzing, chirping sound in the rainforest this morning. What is it? It is the call of a male poison dart frog. First, he pulls air into his vocal **sac**, which makes it grow bigger. Then he pushes the air back out, and it makes a very loud buzzing noise. That sound means he is looking for a mate. It also means that this spot in the rainforest belongs to him. If another male frog tries to move in, the two will wrestle. Whichever frog gives up first is the loser.

Not too far away, a female poison dart frog has heard the call. She wants a mate, too. When she finds the frog she likes, they do a very special dance. She rubs his nose. He circles around her. They dip their heads. They arch their necks. They touch each other's arms. This dance goes on for hours. It is the poison dart frog's courtship!

This frog is calling for a mate.

The poison dart frog mother has tried to lay her eggs in a safe place.

After mating, the female frog finds a wet, safe place to lay dozens of eggs called **spawn**. Wet leaves are best because they form natural bowls to hold rainwater. If there is not enough water to keep the eggs wet, the parents will do the next best thing. They urinate on the eggs!

The eggs are covered in a thick gel to keep them from blowing away or sliding off. For the first 10 weeks, the baby frogs are tadpoles. Over those weeks, they do a lot of changing. Their **gills** disappear. Their tails get smaller and smaller. They grow legs and feet. Even their eyes change position!

This is a poison dart tadpole.

LOOK AGAIN

WHAT BODY PARTS CAN YOU SEE ON THIS TADPOLE THAT ADULT POISON DART FROGS ALSO HAVE?

Male poison dart frogs are very caring dads! As the babies grow, their father returns again and again to check on them. When they are a few weeks old, it is time to move the family. Carefully, the male frog backs up to the tadpoles, and they crawl up onto his back. **Mucus** keeps them from sliding off. Slowly, the father carries the tadpoles to a more protected area like a hole in a dead tree, a pond, or a broken coconut shell. Here the babies are safer from predators.

By the end of 3 months, the tadpoles will be adult frogs and have their bright color patterns. For months they will hunt for food. Then when they're a year old, it will be time for them to send out their own mating calls. ✺

This poison dart frog is carrying tadpoles on its back.

CHAPTER 5

PUTTING THE POISON TO USE

Listen again! Hear that chirping, buzzing noise? Is it a male poison dart frog? Not this time. It is a tribesman of South or Central America. He is standing in the middle of the rainforest and imitating the sound of the tree frogs. He whistles and chirps. The frogs hop and jump to him, thinking he is a frog. When he spots them, he covers his hands with waxy leaves and picks them up. Into a bag they go.

Poison dart frogs are far too small for humans to eat. And they are poisonous. So what do some tribes want

Tribespeople catch frogs like this one to use their toxin.

them for? The name of the frog is an important clue. For many years, these frogs have been captured for the toxin they produce. Tribespeople hold the frogs down with sticks and run the tips of their arrows and darts across the frog's skin. When they are done, they often release the frog back into the wild.

Next, the arrows and darts are put into special **blowguns**. Tribespeople use these to hunt birds, monkeys, jaguars, and other animals. Guns are often too loud and scare away creatures, but blowguns are quiet.

The frogs' venom is used to make darts for blowguns like these.

One golden poison dart frog can provide enough material for 30 to 50 darts. The **toxicity** lasts for up to a year! Over time, fewer and fewer tribes have been using this method. But the tradition has been around for centuries.

The poison produced by these unique frogs may one day also help people. Researchers suspect that instead of causing pain, the toxin may help prevent it. Studies have shown that some frog species produce poison that is 200 times more powerful than morphine. Morphine is one of the medical world's strongest painkillers. Doctors believe the poison can be used to help people with heart and **circulation** problems. Wouldn't it be amazing if poison could actually stop pain?

THINK ABOUT IT

POISON DART FROGS ARE NOT BORN POISONOUS. HOW DOES THIS FACT SUPPORT THE IDEA THAT THE TOXIN COMES FROM THEIR DIET?

THINK ABOUT IT

- In chapter 1, you learned that poison dart frogs are built to be able to climb trees. What may be some of the reasons they would need to climb trees? How would this ability help them?

- What are two of the main clues that the poison these frogs produce comes through their diet?

- Tadpoles are born with gills and tails, but they fade away as they grow. Why do you think they have them in the first place?

- If their poison begins to help people instead of hurt them, it may be time for these colorful frogs to get a new name! Can you suggest another name for them?

LEARN MORE

FURTHER READING

Bredeson, Carmen. *Poison Dart Frogs Up Close.* Berkeley Heights, NJ: Enslow Elementary, 2009.

Dussling, Jennifer. *Deadly Poison Dart Frogs.* New York: Bearport Publishing, 2009.

Ganeri, Anita. *Poison Dart Frog.* North Mankato, MN: Heinemann Read and Learn, 2011.

Kingston, Anna. *The Life Cycle of a Poison Dart Frog.* New York: Gareth Stevens, 2011.

McCarthy, Cecilia Pinto. *Poison Dart Frogs.* North Mankato, MN: Pebble Plus, 2012.

WEB SITES

National Geographic Kids—Poison Dart Frog
http://kids.nationalgeographic.com/animals/poison-dart-frog.html
Read all about the poison dart frog and how it survives in the rainforests.

Rainforest Animals—Poison Dart Frogs
www.rainforestanimals.net/rainforestanimal/poisondartfrog.html
Find out what animals share the rainforest environment with the poison dart frogs.

San Diego Zoo Animals—Poison Frog
http://animals.sandiegozoo.org/animals/poison-frog
Discover fun facts and statistics about all kinds of poison dart frogs, plus visit the frog exhibit at the San Diego Zoo.

GLOSSARY

amphibians (am-FIB-ee-uhnz) cold-blooded vertebrates such as frogs, toads, newts, and salamanders

blowguns (BLOH-guhn) tubes through which darts or arrows are blown by people's breath

circulation (sur-kyuh-LAY-shuhn) the movement of blood through the heart and blood vessels

endangered (en-DAYN-jerd) threatened with a type of danger and/or extinction

gills (GILZ) the breathing organs of water animals

immune (ih-MYOON) protected from physical harm

mucus (MYOO-kuss) a slimy mixture of water and other liquids from glands

paralyze (PAR-uh-lize) to make something unable to move or act

predators (PRED-uh-turz) animals that hunt and eat other animals

prey (PRAY) an animal hunted or taken for food

sac (SAK) a baglike structure on an animal or plant

saliva (suh-LYE-vuh) spit; fluid produced by the salivary glands to aid in eating and digestion

spawn (SPAWN) a mass of eggs produced and deposited by amphibians

species (SPEE-sheez) particular kinds or types of living things

toxicity (tok-SIS-i-tee) the level of how poisonous something is

INDEX